Lamplight Collection of Modern Art

Audubon, Homer, Whistler
and
Nineteenth-Century America

by John Wilmerding

LAMPLIGHT
PUBLISHING

Lamplight Publishing, Inc.
New York, New York

PUBLISHED IN THE UNITED STATES OF AMERICA IN 1975
by Lamplight Publishing, Inc., N.Y. 10016

First published in the series "Mensili d'Arte" Copyright © 1967
by Fratelli Fabbri Editori, Milan, Italy

Illustrations Copyright © 1970 by Fratelli Fabbri Editori, Milan,
Italy on the American Edition.

Library of Congress Catalog Card Number: 70-1066-57

SBN 0-88308-011-7

The nineteenth century is in many respects the most interesting in the history of the shaping and development of art in the United States. It was during this century that many of the themes associated with the American character first appeared. Certain of these ideas—such as the force and vitality of America—are still apparent in the character and art of the country. It would be useful to note some of these themes as they occur and recur through American art of the nineteenth century.

From the beginning the settlers of the New World were conscious of their sense of discovery. Some had left home stimulated by the emerging scientific challenges of the Renaissance, others to escape the social restrictions or religious persecutions of their native lands. Whatever the cause, the newly discovered continent of North America took on qualities of savagery and luxury at the same time, qualities which many foreigners still associate with America.

The early explorers frequently made maps of the regions they visited and drawings of Indian life. The same fascination with documenting new territory and recording native habits would reappear often during this century. Awe of the landscape, fear and excitement at the unknown would motivate painters of the American West like Albert Bierstadt (Plate 21) and Thomas Moran. And after the territories beyond the Mississippi were settled toward the end of the century, others sought to satisfy this desire for the exotic by journeying to new virgin landscapes, as when Frederick Edwin Church and Martin Johnson Heade (Plates 19 and 26) set out in the 1860s for the great mountain ranges of South America, or when Church, James Hamilton, and William Bradford went to the Arctic in the 1870s and eighties.

American artists gave the landscapes they painted a special meaning, as they did the inhabitants they encountered. The life of the American Indian was given as its symbol that of the Noble Savage, an incarnation of brutal force and ideal beauty that was also seen in the environment. Some painters like George Catlin (Plate 28) sought to record the physiognomy and dress of the Indian with the accuracy that a journalist might use.

This pleasure in discovering and charting the unknown existed from the start, as did the American sense of scale and bigness. Of particular interest in nineteenth-century American painting is the development of the panoramic composition as a means of expression. At the beginning of the century the panorama was largely a borrowing of a type of stage entertainment from European artists. Not unlike wall decorations, large expanses of canvases could be unrolled with accompanying commentary or music. Such a presentation was especially effective for the depiction of historical events that needed grandiose scale, high moral justification, and dramatic immediacy. Americans soon discovered these qualities nicely suited their own impressions of the American landscape. As the century progressed, their canvases tended to become larger, in an effort to equate size with grandness. But another subtle dimension was stressed as well: the increasing horizontality of the canvas, in order to suggest the presumably endless openness and breadth of the continent. This aim saw fulfillment in the work of Bierstadt, Church, and others (Plates 20 and 21) during the last half of the century. But it has had its natural extension in much of contemporary art, notably in the large canvases of the Abstract Expressionists and Pop Artists since World War II.

Moreover, along with size went force and dynamism. The blasted tree trunks that appeared in the foregrounds of Thomas Cole's landscapes (Plate 14) told of nature's underlying power and of the divine force that was everywhere immanent. Such details were visible records of the often violent changes wrought by time, reminders that the present had a history behind it.

Americans have long been a pragmatic people, and their art reflects this in its continuing concern with fact and physical presence. One sees this in the eighteenth-century portraits of John Singleton Copley, America's first great painter. Men and women of substance, both professionally and physically, appear solidly and tangibly in Copley's paintings. They bear a sense of weight, and with it mortality, that the artist conveys through loving attention to textures and materials. Winslow Homer (Plates 42 and 43) would also demonstrate this American love of fact. A painter who celebrated exercise and the out-of-doors, as so many of his century and country did, he has often provoked comparison with his Impressionist counterparts in Europe. Certain similarities, due probably more to common period concerns than to any exchange of influences, do exist between Homer's work in the sixties and seventies and that of Boudin or the early Monet. The distinction that is important here is that French Impressionism increasingly led its exponents toward the dissolution of form (guided by the scientific principles of recording only those optical sensations of light and color that hit the retina). Homer, for all of his dedication to capturing on canvas the out-of-doors as he directly saw it, was never willing to sacrifice form for theory. The space in his paintings continued to suggest a three-dimensional depth in which solid objects and figures could stand or move, while Impressionist space became shallower and shallower, until by the end of the century the canvases of Monet and Seurat consisted of almost flat areas of light and color with only the barest resemblance to any recorded spatial reality.

Like their European counterparts, however, American artists responded throughout the nineteenth century to the qualities and meaning of light, especially in landscape painting. Landscape, of course, was especially suited to the interests of both European and American painters, who increasingly left the studio to paint outdoors. The emergence of landscape painting, and the related efforts at the rendering of light, is one of the fundamental developments of the century. Varied as American art was throughout the period, artists repeatedly returned to the relationship of landscape and light. This is evident in the work of the first important figure of the century, Washington Allston.

The Federal Period

Allston represents the first flowering of the romantic movement in America, just as his friend and contemporary John Vanderlyn would be the principal exponent of a continuing classical style. Both men shared certain concerns in common and, like many Americans, traveled to Europe in search of identities to be derived, but also distinct, from Europe. Allston is perhaps typical of the romantic temperament; his work was uneven and irregular, yet in it may be found many of the themes recurring through American art ever since. Coming to maturity in the first decades of the new century, he represented the emerging interest in subjects other than portraiture, which had dominated the colonial world.

Allston painted through the period of transition from the eighteenth-century world, with its interests in mythology, history, and portrait painting, to the nineteenth, with its interests in nature and landscape. The latter is well represented by a major early work, *Storm Rising at Sea,* 1804 (Plate 2). Done while on his first trip to Europe, the painting reflects the high drama of Benjamin West's history pieces and the theatrics of Joseph Vernet's stormy seascapes. Stressing the smallness of the vessels, and of man, in the expanse of a hostile sea, Allston depicts the grand power of nature and man's lonely voyage of life. The need for self-sufficiency and the intimation of mystery are notes that will appear later in the haunting rhythms of Albert P. Ryder's moonlight marines (Plate 51).

Actually, moonlight haunted Allston, too, as his *Moonlit Landscape* testifies (Plate 3). This brooding image came after his second trip abroad, and reflected his admiration for the most painterly of the old masters, Titian, Veronese, and Rubens. In Titian especially Allston discovered a warmth of color and light which he sought to adapt himself. By experimenting with underpainting and glazing he was able to achieve an inner luminosity. Across this glowing landscape, partly remembered from the hills of Rome and partly imagined, unexplained figures proceed out of some dream of classical antiquity into a personal reality of the present.

John Vanderlyn's art also blended the classical and the romantic. In 1803 he joined Allston in Paris; he, like Allston, had been introduced to Benjamin West, the patriarch of American painters, in London. Vanderlyn preferred to base his style on that of the prevailing French Neo-Classicism. His first picture in this style was the historical piece *The Death of Jane McCrea,* 1804 (Plate 5). Taken from one of the more poignant episodes in the American Revolutionary War, the story depicted the massacre by Indians of the pathetic heroine on her wedding day. West himself had set the example of painting contemporary events when in 1771 he painted the *Death of General Wolfe.* Another scene from the American wars, it broke precedent by clothing the figures in contemporary rather than classical costume and in other ways suggesting the immediacy of the event. Like West, Vanderlyn used somewhat classical postures and composition. Here the Indians are based on antique sculpture, and the balanced composition probably derives from the French arbiter of Neo-Classicism, Jacques Louis David, with suggestions of both his *Oath of the Horatii* and *Battle of the Sabines.* The tragedy that Vanderlyn rendered was an appropriate one for crystalizing sentiment against the British, since it was they who had used the Indians in their march south from Canada in 1777. Americans needed to find, even invent, their own immortals, and the ennoblement of events and personalities of the Revolution was the first step. For all its classical allusions, however, *Jane McCrea* is imbued with romantic overtones: from its initial appeal to pathos and emotion to the dark Arcadian forest that stretches off to the right background. There in the distance are the possible rescuers who heighten this gothic tale by not being able to reach the victim in time.

That Vanderlyn was no pure classicist was evident when he too responded to the transcendent beauty of color and light that he discovered in Correggio and Titian. The latter presumably provided a source for Vanderlyn's *Ariadne* of 1814 (Plate 4). Yet here again his obvious debt to classical art and literature was tempered by the romantic luminosity with which he suffused the landscape. In fact, the artist pays as much attention to the natural setting as he does to the nude, the first in American art. Significantly, Vanderlyn sought to include typical American flowers, an effort to satisfy both the ideal and the real. These two demands would grow in intensity during the next three decades, as American taste required that artists both instruct the viewer—hence the propriety of the ideal nude—and depict accurately things American, such as local scenery. It was a dilemma that the next generation would continue to feel, as Asher B. Durand recognized in his own landscapes, and more specifically when he chose to make an engraving after Vanderlyn's painting.

There were other artists in the opening decades of the century whose work showed the increasing variety of subjects painted during this transitional period. One of these was Henry Sargent, whose *Dinner Party* (Plate 11) and a companion painting, *The Tea Party*, both in the Boston Museum of Fine Arts, are charming illustrations of life in America around 1820.

Another painter of the Federalist period, and one of its dominant personalities, was Gilbert Stuart, whose career was already well launched during the last quarter of the eighteenth century. Basing his style on contemporary English models, Stuart achieved a certain popularity abroad in the 1780s before returning to work in America in the next decade. He subsequently produced the pictures by which he is best known, the various portraits of George Washington. Surely one of his most beautiful and evocative portraits is the unfinished one of the poet *Mrs. Perez Morton* (Plate 12).

The loose, free brushwork and the pale tonalities inform the portrait with a feminine grace. Yet beneath this there lies an intimation of the sadness that was to come into her personal life. As a painting it conveys a sense of improvisation, a freshness that was a long way from the stiff formal postures and tight realism of Colonial painting. Its appearance of casualness, along with Stuart's use of colors, brushwork, and composition that were expressly suited to the subject, presage the penetrating portraits by Thomas Eakins, who would find in Walt Whitman another poetic subject for his canvas.

An even more versatile figure, also belonging to both the last part of the eighteenth century and to the early part of the nineteenth, was Charles Willson Peale, who had been a soldier during the American Revolution. Peale, a portraitist, was also interested in science and medicine; his studio was filled with stuffed animals as well as paintings. In 1806 he organized what came to be the Pennsylvania Academy, the first such effort to establish a museum and art gallery in the country. Although the quality of his work was frequently uneven, he produced a remarkable portrait in *Group on a Staircase* of 1795 (Plate 7) depicting his two sons pausing on the curve of the stairs. The realism and palpability of form recall John Singleton Copley, yet the subtle fluidity of design is something new in American art. He cleverly connects the lines of light and shadow with the planes of the steps and the axes of the figures, who themselves are contrasted, one diagonal and rising upward, the other vertical and turning downward. The illusionism represented a bold versatility that would reappear in American art a hundred years later in the *trompe l'oeil* still lifes of William M. Harnet (Plate 48). Peale would duplicate this inventiveness within little over a decade, when he painted his *Disinterment of the Mastodon*, 1806 (Plate 6). As in the work of West, Copley, and Vanderlyn before him, here was history in the making, but none of their high moral drama. Instead, this was a local, personal piece of narration, the first major genre painting in American art, anticipating John Quidor's *The Gold Diggers* of 1832 (Plate 34). Peale himself had organized the digging up of the mammoth's bones in upstate New York following the discovery some years earlier of a thirty-nine-inch long thighbone in the area. It took Peale's numerous assistants three months to exhume the gigantic bones.

The painting that resulted included some fifty figures, of which at least eighteen were portraits. For Peale it was a *tour de force* combining portraiture, genre, history, and landscape painting.

Aside from the artistic legacy that he left, Peale established a family dynasty of painters. Through three generations there were twenty painting Peales, many appropriately named after old masters. One of the most talented was Raphael Peale, Charles Willson's son. Adapting his father's technique of illusionary realism, and doubtless mindful of seventeenth-century Dutch and Italian painting, Raphael produced masterfully composed and rendered still lifes. He could arrange a selection of varied kitchen objects and foods, illuminate textures and juxtapose forms in a manner not unworthy of Chardin (Plate 8). In one still life, *After the Bath*, 1823 (Plate 9), the painting approaches genre but displays a formal abstraction that is strikingly modern.

Charles Willson Peale had shown that the American artist was free to paint local and contemporary subjects of his own interest. National events such as the War of 1812 were to provide their share of topics for artists. Just as the War for Independence produced national heroes, shrines, and myths, so too did the dramatic maritime battles of this latest war.

An English-born painter who took advantage of the opportunity was Thomas Birch. The use of heavy paint, low horizon, and a turbulent setting in his *The United States and the Macedonian* (Plate 1) are reminiscent of the great age of Dutch Baroque painting, which Birch knew well through examples collected by his father and through widely available engravings. At about the same time a young friend of Allston's, Samuel F. B. Morse, painted another picture of national interest, *Congress Hall: Old House of Representatives* (Plate 10). Here is an imposing and elegant interior of Federal architecture as the setting for America's most democratic institution. Regrettably, Morse's great promise as an artist was increasingly frustrated; he turned to fortune in another area and successfully developed the telegraph. (The scientific concerns of American artists should not go unnoted, for Morse belongs to a group including Peale, Audubon, Catlin, Heade, Lane, Bradford, Rimmer, Eakins, and Homer, all of whom were in one way or another preoccupied with scientific methods or instruments.)

The Hudson River School

The first cohesive school of painting in nineteenth-century America was, not surprisingly, built on the work of the landscapists. Nature held special meaning for this romantic movement. Flowering both in literature and art by the 1830s, the spiritual values of Transcendentalism propounded by Emerson and Thoreau confirmed precisely what the painter was after. It was more than coincidental that Emerson's crucial essay *Nature* and Thomas Cole's monumental series on the *Course of Empire* (Plate 15) both appeared in 1836. Cole and his colleague, Thomas Doughty, were the founders of the important Hudson River School, a title loosely given to a whole generation of landscape painters working in upstate New York and northern New England in the 1840s and fifties.

Doughty was the oldest and his landscapes are among the first picturing American scenery. A self-taught artist, he also made use of engravings after English paintings and studied seventeenth-century Dutch art during a trip abroad. Through vibrant textures of pigment and improvisations on what he actually saw his paintings usually evoked the quiet moods of nature and often possessed a pastoral charm. *In Nature's Wonderland* (Plate 13), in which diffused light plays across the various forms of the cliff and the trees that frame the central pool of reflecting water, is such an example.

Thomas Cole's landscapes, like Doughty's, stimulated a sense of contemplation, but in contrast to Doughty's rather generalized forms, Cole worked toward a more precise recording of his setting, as in his famous *Oxbow: the Connecticut River Near Northampton* (Plate 14). Here he employs the device of a panoramic composition, presenting the spectator with a vast sweep of the valley seen from a nearby mountainside. Small figures are barely visible in the foreground, reminding us that they are standing before a divine creation. In fact, evidence of God's handiwork appears prominently in the forms of the torn tree trunks in the foreground and the passing thunderstorm in the background. The former tells of forces more powerful than man's affecting the world around us; the latter shows a natural force in action, the rain cleansing and purifying the land. In this way Cole could satisfy contemporary demands for accuracy in depicting an *American* landscape *and* for elevating art to a nobler, more morally instructive cause. Both causes could be joined under one mission for the artist, namely to save the pristine virtue of American nature before if fell to the desecrations of civilization's touch. This purity was what distinguished the American wilderness from European landscape, which had lost some of its freshness through age, industrialization, and overfamiliarity. Still, the pride of Americans was giving way to fear, as they began to feel that the defilement of their continental landscape was near. The artist, therefore, had a calling that went beyond mere accurate reporting of landscape. A follower of Cole's, Jasper Cropsey, summarized the challenge when he said: "The axe of civilization is busy with our old forests, and artisan ingenuity is fast sweeping away the relics of our national infancy.... Yankee enterprise has little sympathy with the picturesque, and it behooves our artists to rescue from its grasp the little that is left, before it is ever too late."

Dedication to the real and to the ideal presented the two polarities artists of the period were to move within. Cole leaned more to the former in *The Oxbow*; he chose to emphasize the latter for his great series of paintings *The Course of Empire*, 1836. Here was a strident pictorial essay on the folly of human vanity elaborately presented in five sequential paintings. His friend James Fenimore Cooper interpreted the story in a novel written shortly after *(The Crater)*, which reaffirmed the parallel and interlocking concerns of American painters and writers of this generation. The cycle of paintings showed a history of a civilization and its interaction with nature, beginning with *The Savage State*, and followed by *The Pastoral State*, *The Consummation of Empire* (Plate 15), *The Destruction of Empire*, and *Desolation*. Drawing on his knowledge of Salvator Rosa, Claude Lorrain, Poussin, and John Martin, Cole gave unity to the series by including a distant mountain in each painting. Soft lighting suffuses the first painting of man and nature in their primeval condition; the light and dark color contrasts become increasingly strong as the manifestations of civilization begin to cover the landscape; this reaches a violent climax in the painting of nature's revolt and upheaval; then there is a settling back to somber tones for the final evening setting of nature once more without man or his temples. It was an ambitious undertaking, attempted but not equaled again by Cole in a later series devoted to the *Voyage of Life*.

The series was a success with his contemporaries in America, but the direction of the future would lie in works like *The Oxbow*. However modified to accommodate the public's taste for overtones of morality and idealism, Cole's later views of New England and the Catskills embodied the rising flood of attention to specific qualities and details of native scenery.

Cole's colleague Asher B. Durand preferred this aspect of painting. Where Cole advised the painter to sketch the essence of nature's forms, for example, *types* of trees, Durand stressed the precise drawing of specific, individual forms as they were actually encountered in the woods. Part of Durand's precision came from his early training as an engraver, and it is well to note the important role of the graphic arts in the history of American painting. A medium emphasizing expression through line and through tonalities of black and white, printmaking would prove decisive in careers as diverse as those of J. S. Copley, Fitz Hugh Lane, Winslow Homer, and George Bellows. For Durand it made him conscious of composing in terms of dark-light contrasts rather than color. His paintings were accumulations of details and painstaking descriptiveness. One of his great testaments to his friends was *Kindred Spirits* (Plate 17), painted in 1849, the year after Thomas Cole's death, and showing Cole standing in the American wilderness alongside the nature poet William Cullen Bryant.

Two younger painters, both admirers of Cole and exponents of the Hudson River style in the next generation, were Worthington Whittredge and John F. Kensett. Each had had exposure to European art: Whittredge had studied at the recently popular school at Düsseldorf, Germany; Kensett had toured the Continent seeing primarily seventeenth- and eighteenth-century Italian painting. In his *House by the Sea* of 1872 (Plate 16) Whittredge continued the direction set by Cole and Durand toward recording accurately a particular locale, in this case the countryside slightly inland from the beaches of Newport, Rhode Island. Like Cole, Whittredge chose a high point of view and included a sweeping panorama of the seashore landscape. A few years earlier Kensett painted a nearby area of the coast in *Newport Harbor* (Plate 18). Typical of this artist is his shoreline point of view and the subtle balance of a large mass of rocks on one side of the composition with the open water and sky on the other side. Both artists exhibit a preciseness of drawing that suits the clarity of their vision. Most significant of all, though, is the similarity of the light and atmosphere that suffuse both pictures. While each painter achieves a sense of a specific time of day, he also suggests timelessness.

The undisputed masters of the second generation of the Hudson River School were Albert Bierstadt and Frederick Edwin Church. Moving out of the, by now, well-painted confines of New England, these two sought fresh territory in the western United States or South America and the Arctic. Bierstadt was a native of Germany, but was brought up in New Bedford, Massachusetts. As a youth he returned to Düsseldorf for training in its tight, rather melodramatic manner of painting. Düsseldorf was also to attract Sanford Gifford, George Caleb Bingham, and Eastman Johnson (Plates 31 and 38). Bierstadt was back in New Bedford in 1857 and for the next couple of decades made several journeys to the western United States. Traveling through the Plains, Rocky Mountains, and territories now in national parks, he made extensive sketches from which many of his best paintings were subsequently derived. One of these is the great *Rocky Mountains*, 1863 (Plate 21), in which one can see an extension of Cole's concern with the cosmic grandeur of nature. Here on an almost grandiose scale, although with a microscopic attention to detail, Bierstadt's canvas attempted to approximate the vision of this new American wilderness. Artists like Bierstadt were overwhelmed by the plenitude and grandeur that they saw, whether in millions of roaming bison and flights of birds, or in the sweep of the plains and towering heights of the mountains. It was no wonder that the Hudson was likened to the Rhine, the Mississippi to the Nile, or the Rockies to the Alps. America had its own drama.

Bierstadt's strongest rival of the 1860s and seventies was Frederick Edwin Church, who was equally concerned with the force and grandeur of nature. His first major work was *Niagara Falls*, 1857 (Plate 19), a wonder of the continent that had attracted numbers of painters before him: Vanderlyn, John Trumbull, Alvan Fisher, Morse, and Kensett. But Church's version presented something new, an aspect placing it distinctively in the second half of the nineteenth century — the close-in vantage point and the horizontality of the composition. Rather than standing back from the subject, the spectator has to move in to the very precipice of the falls. He is confronted with its pulsing power. The water sweeps in from one side of the canvas and out the other, as if the dimensions of the picture cannot contain this great event. Church also emphasizes the horizon, placing rising clouds just above it to suggest that the scene extends even beyond the sight of the viewer. Thus Niagara Falls is more than just a tourist attraction, a picturesque scene — it becomes a symbol of the American wilderness itself. *Niagara Falls* met with immediate success when it was first exhibited. No wonder. It satisfied all the demands for an American painting that critics and public could appreciate. Pleased and stimulated, Church set off in the next decade to paint the rain forests of Jamaica, the great mountain ranges of South America, the icebergs of the Arctic, and the ancient cities of the Aegean and Near East. Each subject in its way was for the artist an embodiment of history and time. He found his special symbols of power in thunderstorms, rainbows, volcanic eruptions, even the sun and light itself. Whether mountains of rock or ice, each in its naturalness was a record of geologic time, but also a pristine sublimity to be discovered for the first time. *Secluded Landscape at Sunset* (Plate 20), painted a few years after *Niagara Falls,* contained all the ingredients of the wilderness iconography. Based on sketches Church had done along the rocky Maine coast, the painting includes not only familiar young and old trees, worn and sharp mountains, but also a sunset worthy of any god's creation. It was an almost miraculous recording of an actual scientific phenomenon as well as a pictorial incarnation of nature's spiritual content. The extraordinary daring of clashing the reds and yellows in this drama make clear that by 1860, the date of its execution, American artists were giving *light* a very special and significant role in their paintings.

The Luminists

Light had also taken on distinctive meaning for Church's contemporaries Fitz Hugh Lane and Martin Johnson Heade, often called "luminist" painters. While their interests were similar to those of the French Impressionists, the aims of the Americans were modified by their rather different attitudes toward nature. Light, as we have seen, was both a physical and a spiritual presence. One of Lane's predecessors and an influence on his work was Robert Salmon. Like Cole, Salmon was born in England, though he did not sail to the United States until 1828. Primarily a marine painter, he settled and worked almost entirely around Boston, its streets, wharves, harbor, and islands. As a marine painter his work presents an interesting parallel to the better-known landscapes of Cole. At his best Salmon could imbue a painting with a crystalline luminosity, as he does in his *Boston Harbor as Seen from Constitution Wharf* (Plate 22). A narrative record of the lively events in an increasingly busy port, it also possesses a firm sense of design and a sensitive feeling for the quality of glowing light and atmosphere.

At work in a Boston lithography shop during Salmon's last years in Boston, the young Fitz Hugh Lane adapted many of Salmon's characteristics in his own painting. Also a recorder of life in the harbors and along the coast of New England, Lane moved progressively toward more simplified compositions and an evocative poetry of light. A potentially colorless scene in his own native harbor became the subject of *Ships Stuck in Ice off Ten Pound Island, Gloucester* (Plate 25), which Lane has enlivened with a convincing sense of atmosphere and a variety of tonal changes within the limited range of winter colors. Characteristically, he has grouped the two largest vessels slightly off center, while focusing attention on them with the several smaller boats and figures standing on the ice nearby.

In the 1850s and sixties Lane made regular summer cruises down the Maine coast. On several occasions he sketched extensively around the island of Mount Desert, which Frederick Church was visiting in the same years. It is not known whether they met there, but both men began to show greater consciousness of light effects in their work at this time. Coming from one of these trips was Lane's view of *Owl's Head, Maine* (Plate 24), done in 1863, not long after Church's *Sunset.* Lane obviously preferred a quieter, more lyrical mode of expression, stressing open expanses, as here in the pale morning sky. He used subdued, understated colors, and painted them on very thinly. As was so typical of his mature work, *Owl's Head* achieves a special feeling of detachment, contemplation, and solitude. Lane views nature in careful detail but he also transforms it into something timeless and spiritual.

Martin Johnson Heade's work is often closely associated with Lane's, and for good reason. He was a friend of Church's and almost certainly knew Lane, too. Heade's painting had two very distinctive styles, seen in *Spring Showers, Connecticut Valley,* and *Approaching Storm, Narragansett Bay* (Plates 27 and 26). In the first he used the paler, lyrical colors seen frequently in Lane's late work, but fills the scene with a heavier atmosphere. In a manner that became characteristic of Heade he has arranged forms in terms of their silhouettes, as here, for example, in the rounded shapes of the trees seen against the green hillside. It is an optimistic and bright picture in contrast to the threatening, somber note of *Approaching Storm.* In this Heade suggests an intense foreboding and romantic mystery that recalls Allston's *Moonlit Landscape* while it anticipates Albert Ryder's *Toilers of the Sea* (Plate 51). Particularly effective are the incisive drawing of details and surreal clarity of white forms against the black setting. As light was able to reveal a special quality of place in Kensett's and Whittredge's paintings of Newport (Plates 18 and 16), here Heade chooses the power of darkness for his view of nearby Narragansett Bay.

In the hands of men like Lane, Heade, Church, and Bierstadt, American landscape painting had achieved an important place in the history of art by mid-nineteenth century. There were other subjects, however, that were to provide means of expression for the artists of this youthful nation.

John James Audubon brought to his well-publicized paintings of American birds and animals the same scientific passion that Heade had shown in a series of his paintings of North and South American hummingbirds and that had likewise motivated Church to record the spectacular details of South American mountains. Audubon's mature watercolors possess a crisp, linear style, as seen in the striking *White Gerfalcon* (Plate 23). Masterfully exploiting the expressive potential of the bird's silhouette, he juxtaposes the bird in flight and at rest. Varying the pose and setting for every creature he painted, Audubon was able to capture the unique qualities of each species. George Catlin had a similar interest in capturing for posterity the habits and dress of the American Indian (Plate 28).

Genre Painting

Another type of painting that was flourishing by mid-century was that of genre, scenes of everyday life. Three of the most prominent figures here were John Quidor, William Sidney Mount, and George Caleb Bingham. Together they give a colorful picture of the enthusiastic optimism bred by Jacksonian Democracy. Andrew Jackson's election to the Presidency in 1829 signaled a new era of the common man, and with it a consciousness of nationality and the workings of democratic institutions, as well as an awareness of one's environment.

Quidor was the most literary of these three genre painters, though as a contemporary of Cole and Durand, this is no surprise. While he took some of his early themes from biblical and romantic literature, for example Cervantes and Spenser, he drew most heavily on his American friends James Fenimore Cooper and Washington Irving. With great humor and fantasy he transformed his pictures from mere illustrations of stories into imaginative, expressive compositions. One is the wild night scene of *The Gold Diggers,* 1832 (Plate 34), taken from Irving's *Tales of a Traveller.* Trees and figures gesture with equal animation. The fire and half-obscured moon provide dramatic illumination. The gaping black hole sets off the highlighted arabesques of branches, faces, and fingers. Quidor knew well the language of the gothic tale.

Another Irving work provided the source for *The Return of Rip Van Winkle* (Plate 29). Rip has wakened from his twenty years sleep to return home unrecognized. Each face is a masterful study of character, while gesture and posture again animate the painting. Picturesque local details like the sign with George Washington's image and the American flag fill the background. More curious are the figures of Rip at the center and the youth leaning against the tree, the former strangely reminiscent of Michelangelo's *God the Father,* the latter of his *Bound Slave.* Although there is no evidence that Quidor was familiar with European art, it is conceivable that he did have access to engraved reproductions. In any case his technical control over line and color admirably suited these witty, personal narrations.

Mount's paintings were also replete with humorous narratives. A recently discovered masterpiece is his *Cider Making,* 1841 (Plate 30). The painting is filled with incidents, small events subtly related to each other. Set against the glowing fall landscape of eastern Long Island, Mount's neighbors and friends are engaged in crushing the apples, storing and sampling the cider. He places the figures in groups of three or four alongside contrasting shapes of architecture or barrels. Even the artist himself has a place here — talking to two associates across the fence at the far right. The gaiety in the faces of the participants is mirrored in the bright landscape and warm sunlight. Mount refined his sense of light and composition in *Eel Spearing at Setauket* (Plate 33) of a few years later. Once more the subjects were local friends of his, now fishing in the limpid waters off a farm near the artist's birthplace. Enclosed within the classical triangle made by the spear and paddle, the figures are similarly caught in the serenity of quiet air and water. With its golden light the painting achieves the same suspension of time found in Lane's *Owl's Head* (Plate 24).

It is more than coincidence that George Caleb Bingham painted *Fur Traders Going Down the Missouri* (Plate 32) in the same year as *Eel Spearing*. Rather than Long Island, the subject is now the Mid-West, the great rivers of the Mississippi and Missouri belonging to Mark Twain's Huck Finn and Tom Sawyer. But the same confluence of light and atmosphere enfolds the fur trappers as they quietly glide along with their reflections. Bingham encloses the figures within the larger shapes of the dark trees and billowing clouds in the background. He chronicles life in America with a buoyant optimism at the same time that he removes his subjects to a plane of detached tranquility.

The *Fur Traders* began a decade of unparalleled work for Bingham, and he followed with a series of raftboatmen paintings. *Raftsmen Playing Cards*, 1847 (Plate 31), is one example, with a large group of figures carefully arranged in a central pyramid. Using varied tones of red, yellow, and blue, and repeated shapes and lines, Bingham integrates his figures with the river setting. He would lose much of the restraint and understatement of the boatmen paintings in the late 1850s after a visit to Europe and study at the Düsseldorf School. But in the 1840s his paintings embodied the exuberant vitality of America. He was painting his fellow countrymen in much the same way that Frederick Church was painting their landscapes.

Primitive Painting

Academic painters like Bingham make an interesting contrast with the indigenous folk artist, who was working throughout much of the nineteenth century quite independent of professional schools, art academies, or imported European collections. He was not interested in perspective, single light sources, three-dimensional modeling, or realistic scale. He tended to compose with flat color areas, repeated patterns or lines, and evocative rhythms. Theirs was largely a decorative tradition, and many folk artists were professional decorators of walls, signboards, mantelpieces, furniture, and even birth certificates. Some painted in their own conceptual way the same subjects that interested academic colleagues. For a comparison see the primitive Thomas Chambers' rendering of *The* Constitution *and the* Guerriere (Plate 35), with its bright, opaque colors and patterned line, and the academically trained Thomas Birch's painting of a similar subject (Plate 1), both taken from an event of the War of 1812.

Edward Hicks was a primitive artist who was deeply concerned with Quaker teachings of peace. A favorite theme to which he returned over and over again was *The Peaceable Kingdom* (Plate 36), taken from Isaiah's speech in the Bible about the lion lying down with the lamb. The animals and doll-like figures have a naïve charm not unlike the modern French primitive painter Henri Rousseau. But perhaps the greatest fantasy in conception and execution was the *Historic Monument of the American Republic* (Plate 37) by Erastus Salisbury Field. Also interested in Biblical themes, Field in this instance chose to commemorate the celebration of the country's centennial in 1876. A reflection of the bizarre eclecticism that had characterized American architecture throughout the nineteenth century, it was also intended as a panorama consisting of the major personalities and events in American history. Each is represented by a statue or a carving in one of niches of the towers. At the top, bridges link the turrets together, a symbolic representation of America's growing industrialization.

In the same years that Field was working on his remarkable *Monument*, Eastman Johnson was producing a series of fresh, Impressionistic landscapes on Nantucket Island, Massachusetts (Plate 38). This unpretentious view by Johnson of a group of cranberry pickers in the field combines the nineteenth century's interest in landscape and in the everyday affairs of ordinary people.

Johnson had had some training in a Boston lithography shop, followed by a couple of years in Düsseldorf. These experiences gave him a sense of line and the ability to work in terms of light and dark, which is apparent in his Nantucket landscapes. There is the familiar attention to the poetry of light, linking him to the work of the same period by Heade, Church, and Bierstadt (Plates 26, 20, and 21). Johnson's brushwork, however, is looser, more painterly and suggestive, and has something of the immediacy of Monet's and Boudin's painting of the 1870s.

Homer and Eakins

Winslow Homer, one of the giants in nineteenth-century American art, also devoted attention to landscape and genre. Like Johnson, he had trained briefly in a lithographer's shop, and had vowed at age twenty-one never to work for anyone again.

As an artist, he grew slowly. He recorded army life during the Civil War and made a brief trip to Paris in 1866. He began to paint watercolors in the seventies, and soon showed a grasp of the medium unparalleled up to that time in America. It was a perfect medium for the out-of-doors, as Constable and Turner had discovered a generation earlier in England. The necessary swiftness of execution, the fluid transparencies of the paint, and the brilliant white of the paper were all suited to the desired effects of sunlight and specific weather conditions. At this time Homer was painting during the summers at Gloucester, Massachusetts, and some of his most delightful scenes are of youths playing along the shores and wharves of this vacation coastline. His well-known *Breezing Up*, 1876 (Plate 43), summarizes his love of the outdoors, exercise, and youth. The spectator is invited directly into the painting by the strong diagonal of the sail and mast. The opposing diagonal shapes of the perched figures, the foaming waves, and the intense colors contribute to the subject's vitality.

By the end of the decade Homer had fully explored this style and subject matter. Perhaps in search of new material and a change of scene, he again journeyed to Europe, this time to England, in the spring of 1881. For a year and a half he spent most of his time at the town of Tynemouth on the rugged coast of the North Sea. A marked, even dramatic, change occurred in his work. Painting almost entirely in watercolor, he gave to his work a new monumentality and seriousness. The colors are more somber and more subtle, the brushwork is broader, looser, and more expressive, the compositions more open and powerful. Correspondingly, Homer's subjects are no longer young children at play or vacationers at leisure, but hardy fishermen and their families struggling to make their livelihood in a harsh environment.

He returned to the United States in late 1882, and in the decade that followed produced a series of major paintings dealing with the forces of nature and man's struggle for survival. He settled for much of his life on the lonely coast of Maine at Prout's Neck, where he could continue to experience the brute force of water, weather, and rocky cliffs. All his later work in one way or another takes up the theme of natural survival. One of the best known is *The Gulf Stream*, 1899 (Plate 42). Here Homer uses a composition somewhat like *Breezing Up*, but there are significant differences in the theme of the work, which is typical of his painting after his trip to England in 1881. A single figure lies alone on his boat, the sail and mast lost, while sharks circle about nearby and a waterspout threatens in the distance. The struggle of man, animal, and nature is dramatically apparent. Homer's earlier themes of enjoyment have fully yielded to the most serious ones of the human condition itself.

Another artist who painted in Gloucester briefly was William Morris Hunt. He was a sophisticated, cosmopolitan painter, brother of the fashionable architect Richard Morris Hunt, and a traveler who was welcome in the international circles of Europe. His 1877 view of *Gloucester Harbor* (Plate 39) is the only one of his landscape scenes of that area that he felt captured any sense of real outdoor light. Its loose brushwork and bright, translucent colors do suggest the tangibility of light and atmosphere that was so much a concern of Hunt and his contemporaries.

The reality of light and air transfix the eye in *Max Schmitt in a Single Scull* (Plate 40), painted by Thomas Eakins in 1871. Here the artist shows his friend and himself (in the background) out rowing on the Schuylkill River at Philadelphia on a clear summer afternoon. The painting demonstrates the artist's deep concern with careful drawing, understanding of anatomy, and the sense of time. Here the brilliant light and clear air suggest the suspension of time, confirmed by the figures themselves, who seem to have glanced up momentarily from their rowing. This stilled action reminds us of the camera's eye, an instrument of which Eakins made use. His familiarity with medicine, mathematics, and photography recalls the earlier scientific bents of Charles Willson Peale and Samuel F. B. Morse, and reminds us in addition that the nineteenth century was one fascinated with the development and use of industrial instruments such as the telescope, microscope, camera, typewriter, sewing machine, and telegraph. Many of these machines would affect the ways in which men communicate with each other, but perhaps the most significant was the camera and its influence on how the painter saw. It made him freshly conscious of reality and time. In *Max Schmitt* there is a sense of stopped time and motion, and the clarity of details is such that the scene might have been recorded by a camera. Of course, what makes Eakins a great painter and not merely a photographic recorder is his profound understanding of humanity. As much a lover of exercise and the out-of-doors as was Homer, Eakins also created a picture of a passing era in American history as well as the passage of summer into autumn.

Eakins' uncompromising insistence on honesty led in 1866 to dismissal from his teaching position at the Pennsylvania Academy for removing the loincloth from a nude in a life-drawing class. Victorian Americans were not ready to accept or appreciate such modernity; nor could they accept the graphic realism of his greatest painting — and one considered by many to be the greatest painting ever done by an American artist — *The Gross Clinic* of 1875 (Plate 41), which was rejected as disgusting and offensive to the sensibilities of contemporary viewers. Caught in the strong white light stands Dr. Gross, one of the most eminent physicians of his time. Recalling Rembrandt's *Anatomy Lesson*, this drama of light and dark reflected Eakins' admiration of the heroic realism in seventeenth-century painting. His personal concern for human mortality is again apparent in the powerful depiction of Gross himself, who attends the ritual of life and death in the operating theater. The vigorous brushwork, the firm accents of light, and the vivid redness of blood might be unpleasant, but they are also frank conveyors of the weight of existence.

Naturally, Eakins was bitterly disappointed over the successive rejections of this painting and its later companion, *The Agnew Clinic* of 1889. The further unhappiness of his dismissal drove him from the painting of sports subjects that he had done in the 1870s to concentrating on portraiture. In his later paintings he depicted the appearance and character of his sitters, capturing their distinctive qualities with the right sense of gesture, posture, and expression. For the most part his subjects were professionals like himself, usually creative, contemplative individuals. One of his deepest friendships was with Walt Whitman, who like the artist was a celebrator of life in poetry that was as modern as was Eakins' painting.

The Expatriates

Eakins was misunderstood by the people of his time; John Singer Sargent was enormously admired. Although he, too, responded to the dramatic brushwork and lighting of Velazquez' painting, Sargent preferred to exploit his natural technical virtuosity. This is evident in two of his most acclaimed paintings, *Madame X* (Plate 46) and the *Daughters of Edward Darley Boit*, which possess a boldness of design and subtlety of lighting, but are lacking in that profound revelation of character seen in Eakins' work. Sargent was more at home traveling in fashionable European circles than he was in dreary industrial America, and his portraits appealed to a gilded age that refused to accept the reality of Eakins' world. At their best, his paintings have a dashing boldness; at their weakest, a flashy superficiality.

Along with Sargent, Mary Cassatt and James A. M. Whistler were expatriate painters who followed the compulsion to immerse themselves in avant-garde styles of European art. A friend of Degas and the Impressionists, Mary Cassatt adapted their style to her favorite subject of mother and child (Plate 47), a subject she treated with a special tenderness and delicacy. She also turned out a series of extraordinarily subtle and beautiful etchings. Whistler also knew the Impressionists, and faced in his own oils and etchings many of the problems that they had raised. Probably best known for his association with the "art for art's sake" movement, he brought an originality and independence to his work that anticipate much of twentieth-century art. Flamboyant, egocentric, and self-reliant, Whistler was the image of the modern artist. His painting of *Miss Alexander* (Plate 45) was one of several of a series subtitled "Symphonies in White," an allusion to music that was intended to show that the art of painting was more than just illustration, but was an arrangement of forms, colors, and harmonies that had their own aesthetic delight. Thus he called his paintings arrangements in gray or white or blue, or symphonies, or nocturnes. They were embodiments of abstract feelings and were composed according to internally harmonious arrangements. Whistler's abstractions paralleled and were a part of the new directions taken by Impressionists and Post-Impressionists in France. He was one of the few Americans who understood and contributed significantly to these new directions, and it would be several decades before other American artists could grasp these implications fully.

American painters throughout the nineteenth century loved to depict fact and substance, and while it is a striking contrast to Whistler's painting, the *trompe l'oeil* realism of his contemporaries Harnett and Haberle is no great surprise. Their still-life paintings (Plates 48 and 49) are convincingly deceptive illusions, worthy successors to the carefully arranged compositions of Raphael Peale (Plates 8 and 9).

The Visionaries

The artistic cross-currents of the late nineteenth century are many and not readily sorted out. By contrast to the objective reality seen in Harnett, Homer, and Eakins, Albert Pinkham Ryder was a painter of subjective reality. He painted nature in simplified patterns of flat color areas, and because he had eye trouble he was moved naturally to paint images that were partly derived from memory and the subconscious. He drew widely on contemporary and past romantic literature, as well as the Bible and the plays of Shakespeare. The subject for one painting taken from the Bible was *Jonah* (Plate 50), wherein the swirling paint and churning forms are appropriate to an entirely personal interpretation of the story. Jonah and the whale are caught in the rhythmic convulsions of the water, while the figure of God looms above in clouds that suggest angel wings.

Much of the haunting depth and richness of Ryder's paintings derive from his technical methods, which involved complex underpainting, glazing, and repainting. He often mixed incompatible materials that have since darkened or cracked, yet they produce strange luminosities that well suit his contemplative subjects. One of his favorite themes was the sea, which resulted in a number of paintings with the title *Toilers of the Sea* (Plate 51). With rhythmic flowing lines and repeated silhouettes, these small pictures effectively conveyed Ryder's visions of eternity. Unlike his contemporary artists he went to Europe several times, not for the art, museums, or landscapes abroad, but for the experience of traveling at sea. Its vastness, symbolic of eternity, provided a setting for man's voyage of life.

An artist often associated with Ryder is Ralph Blakelock, whose moonlit landscapes (Plate 52) were the terrestrial equivalent of Ryder's marines. The romantic strain in American art had several exponents in the closing years of the century. Along with Ryder and Blakelock were also George Inness, William Page, Elihu Vedder, and William Rimmer. Inness's art had the most logical and consistent development, from an early Hudson River manner to the development during the 1860s of a personal style that stressed careful composition and the portrayal of weather conditions. In a mature work, *The Coming Storm* (Plate 57), one can see evidence of his preoccupation with a carefully defining foreground, middleground, and background. He felt that these areas should be kept in delicate balance, and that the human figure should not interrupt the horizon line lest it conflict with the landscape as a subject.

Page was attempting similar resolutions in his portraits. The portrait of his wife (Plate 59) was based on a complex system of quadrants, which helped to maintain all parts of the figure in proper proportion to each other and to the surrounding setting. The painting has a strange mystery about it, whether from the quiet stare of his wife or the oddly empty space around her. An enigmatic stillness also haunts Vedder's *Listening to the Sphinx* (Plate 55). Here amidst the ruins of history a seeker of truth comes to learn the riddle of the sphinx. But the explanations and clarifications do not interest Vedder. Dream and melancholy are his themes, as they were much earlier for Allston (Plate 2). They also preoccupied William Rimmer, a doctor, teacher, and frustrated sculptor. Rimmer's remarkable sculptures, drawings, and paintings were images of suffering, symbols of his own (and man's) struggle with cruelty, bestiality, and death. In the empty halls of an unknown building two figures flee; *Flight and Pursuit* (Plate 54) takes place in the corridors of Rimmer's mind.

These imaginative artists were America's most creative figures at century's end. One final group is important, however, because they illustrate the American painter's continuing obsession with Europe. John Twachtman and Childe Hassam were among many who clearly attempted to follow the innovations of the French Impressionists. Both men traveled and studied abroad, and while both made use of Impressionist color and brushwork, they were typical of the "American Impressionists" in that their work did not exactly parallel that of their French counterparts. Still, Twachtman's work (Plate 53) has a subdued lyrical quality that expresses his personal mood as much as any visual reality. Childe Hassam also catches a distinctive mood in his painting of Boston (Plate 58). Hassam, an equally good watercolorist and an even better graphic artist, was at his best in conveying particular qualities of outdoor light, whether brilliant sunshine or misty overcast.

Germany also continued to have an interest for American artists, and by the 1870s Munich had replaced Düsseldorf as a favored place to study. Courbet and seventeenth-century Dutch painting were the principal influences here in the teaching of a new realism. Two American painters who settled here for a few years in the early seventies were Frank Duveneck and William Merritt Chase. In the manner of the Munich masters their paintings exhibited the somber palette of earth colors, so-called crude subject matter, direct execution without preliminary drawings, and immediate, bravura effects. Duveneck's *Child's Portrait* (Plate 60) is a perfect example. It has the typical strong lighting, quick characterization of the sitter, and a sensuousness of paint that are appropriate for achieving the desired effect of spontaneity.

Chase emerged from his German stay a fashionable portraitist, not too unlike Sargent. His later work gradually became more impressionistic, and *A Friendly Visit* (Plate 56) has a charming freshness and intimacy. More important, perhaps, are Chase's contributions to American art as a teacher. In the 1890s he taught at the Art Students League in New York, the Pennsylvania Academy, and at his own schools in New York City and on eastern Long Island. The young Robert Henri, soon to be a part of the first major movement in twentieth-century American art, was a teacher at Chase's school. In 1904 George Bellows arrived from the Midwest to study under Chase and Henri. With John Sloan and others, these younger painters continued the dark, direct manner of painting from Duveneck's and Chase's examples. They also concentrated on the plain, unrefined figures of the everyday scene for their subjects. But they were unequivocally twentieth-century artists, concerned with the city rather than the country. Urban life and its attendant problems—crowding, technology, industry, mechanization—were their themes. Just as the river valleys, the mountains, and the plains had provided subjects for the previous century, the city was the subject of the new. Following Sloan, Henri, and Bellows would come Edward Hopper, Charles Sheeler, and John Marin painting in the thirties and forties. Chase and Duveneck were both stepping stones to the art of the new century. In their paintings was something of an older nostalgia and innocence along with a newer honesty and directness. But above all they project the vitality and creativity that continues in American art today.

PLATES

The Federal Period

PLATE 1 THOMAS BIRCH *Naval Battle Between the* UNITED STATES *and the* MACEDONIAN *on October 30, 1812,* 1813 (71.2 x 87.7 cm) Philadelphia, Historical Society of Pennsylvania

19

20

PLATE 2 WASHINGTON ALLSTON *Storm Rising at Sea*, 1804 (129.5 x 174 cm) Boston, by kind permission of the Museum of Fine Arts, Everett Fund

PLATE 3 WASHINGTON ALLSTON *Moonlit Landscape* (61 x 89 cm) Boston, by kind permission of the Museum of Fine Arts (Gift of W. S. Bigelow)

21

PLATE 4 JOHN VANDERLYN *Ariadne Abandoned on the Island of Naxos*, 1814 (173 x 221 cm) Philadelphia, by kind permission of the Pennsylvania Academy of Fine Arts

PLATE 5   JOHN VANDERLYN *The Death of Jane McCrea,* 1804 (19.2 x 67.3 cm) Hartford, Conn., Wadsworth Atheneum

PLATE 6 CHARLES WILLSON PEALE *Disinterment of the Mastodon,* 1806–1808 (127 x 158.8 cm) Baltimore, Peale Museum (Gift of Mrs. Harry White in memory of her husband)

PLATE 7 CHARLES WILLSON PEALE *Group on a Staircase*, 1795 (226 x
100 cm) Philadelphia, Museum of Art, George W. E. Elkins
Collection (Photo: A. J. Wyatt)

PLATE 8   RAPHAEL PEALE *Still Life*, c. 1820 (47 x 56 cm) Toledo, Ohio, Museum of Art

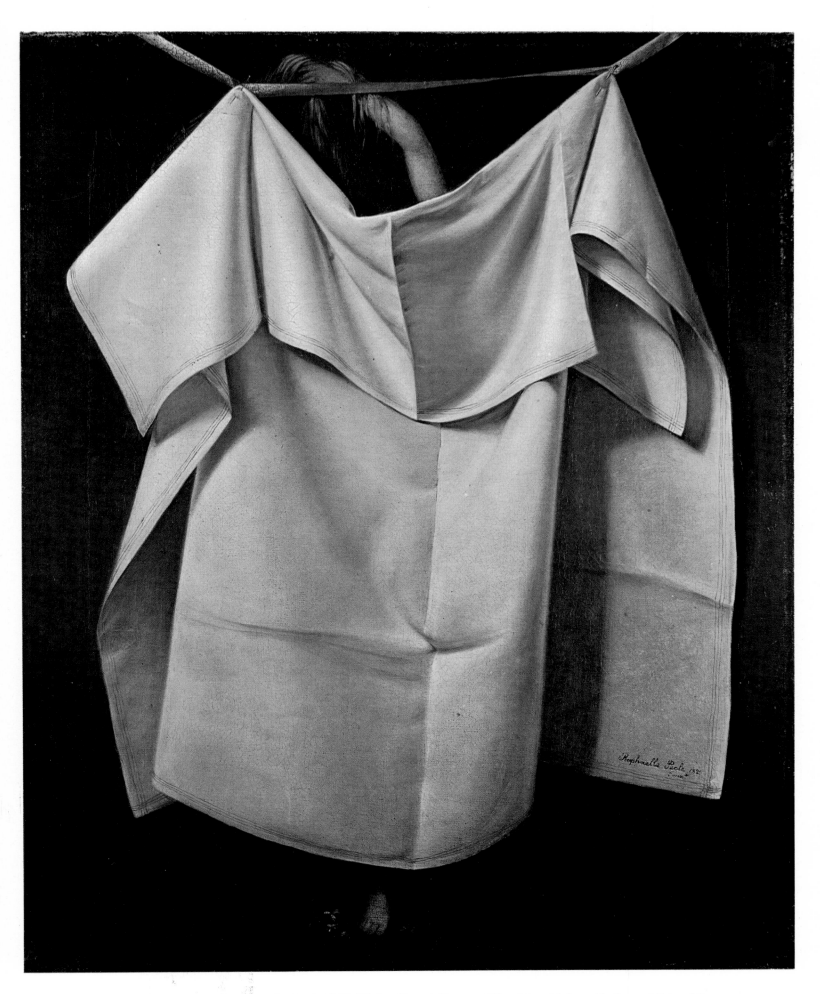

PLATE 9 RAPHAEL PEALE *After the Bath,* 1823 (73.6 x 61 cm) Kansas City, Mo., Nelson Gallery, Atkins Museum

PLATE 10   SAMUEL F. B. MORSE *Congress Hall: Old House of Representatives*, 1822 (219.7 x 332.1 cm) Washington, D.C., Corcoran Gallery of Art

PLATE 11   HENRY SARGENT *Dinner Party* (150.5 x 121.5 cm) Boston, by kind permission of the Museum of Fine Arts
(Gift of Mrs. Horatio A. Lamb)

PLATE 12   GILBERT STUART *Mrs. Perez Morton* (74 x 61.3 cm) Worcester, Mass., Art Museum

Hudson River School

PLATE 13   THOMAS DOUGHTY *In Nature's Wonderland*, 1835 (61.5 x 76.2 cm) Detroit, Institute of Arts

PLATE 14 THOMAS COLE *Oxbow: The Connecticut River Near Northampton*, 1846 (130.8 x 193 cm) New York, Metropolitan Museum of Art

PLATE 15   THOMAS COLE *Course of Empire: The Consummation,* 1836 (129.5 x 193 cm) New York, New-York Historical Society

33

PLATE 16   WORTHINGTON WHITTREDGE *House by the Sea,* 1872 (90 x 135.9 cm) Andover, Mass., Addison Gallery of American Art, Phillips Academy

PLATE 17   ASHER BROWN DURAND *Kindred Spirits,* 1849 (111.8 x 91.5 cm) New York, New York Public Library

PLATE 18   JOHN FREDERICK KENSETT *Newport Harbor*, Chicago, Art Institute of Chicago

36

PLATE 19 FREDERICK EDWIN CHURCH *Niagara Falls*, 1857 (107.9 x 229.9 cm) Washington, D.C., Corcoran Gallery of Art

PLATE 20   FREDERICK EDWIN CHURCH *Secluded Landscape at Sunset*, 1860 (101.6 x 162.5 cm) Cleveland, Ohio, Museum of Art, Mr. and Mrs. William H. Harlett Fund

PLATE 21   ALBERT BIERSTADT *Rocky Mountains*, 1863 (186 x 306.7 cm) New York, Metropolitan Museum of Art

The Luminists

PLATE 22   ROBERT SALMON *Boston Harbor as Seen from Constitution Wharf,* 1829 (68.6 x 104 cm) Annapolis, United States Naval Academy

40

PLATE 23 JOHN JAMES AUDUBON *White Gerfalcons* (96.5 x 63.5 cm) New York, New-York Historical Society

PLATE 24 FITZ HUGH LANE *Owl's Head, Maine,* 1863 (40.6 x 66 cm) Boston, by kind permission of the Museum of Fine Arts, Karolik Collection

PLATE 25 FITZ HUGH LANE *Ships Stuck in Ice off Ten Pound Island, Gloucester,* 1850 (30.5 x 50.1 cm) Boston, by kind permission of the Museum of Fine Arts, Karolik Collection

PLATE 26 Martin Johnson Heade *Approaching Storm, Narragansett Bay*, 1860 (71.1 x 148 cm) Boston, by kind permission of the Museum of Fine Arts, Karolik Collection

44

PLATE 27   MARTIN JOHNSON HEADE *Spring Showers, Connecticut Valley*, 1868 (50.8 × 101.6 cm) Boston, by kind permission of the Museum of Fine Arts, Karolik Collection

45

PLATE 28   GEORGE CATLIN *The Dakota Chief: One Horn*, 1832 (71.1 x 58.4 cm) Chicago, National History Museum

46

Genre Painting

PLATE 29   JOHN QUIDOR *The Return of Rip Van Winkle*, 1829 (139.4 x 158.1 cm) Washington, D.C., National Gallery of Art,
Andrew Mellon Collection

PLATE 30   WILLIAM SIDNEY MOUNT *Cider Making*, 1841 (68.6 x 86.7 cm) New York, Metropolitan Museum of Art (Bequest of Charles Allen Munn)

48

PLATE 31 GEORGE CALEB BINGHAM *Raftsmen Playing Cards,* 1847 (71.1 x 91.4 cm) St. Louis, Mo., City Art Museum, Ezra Linley Fund

PLATE 32   GEORGE CALEB BINGHAM *Fur Traders Going Down the Missouri*, c. 1845 (73.7 x 92.7 cm) New York, Metropolitan Museum of Art

PLATE 33   WILLIAM SIDNEY MOUNT *Ed Spearing at Setauket*, 1845 (91.4 x 73.6 cm) Cooperstown, N.Y., New York State Historical Association

51

PLATE 34   John Quidor *The Gold Diggers,* 1832 (42.5 x 54.6 cm) New York, Brooklyn Museum (Gift of Mr. and Mrs. Bradley Martin)

Primitive Painting

PLATE 35   THOMAS CHAMBERS *The* CONSTITUTION *and the* GUERRIERE, c. 1845 (63 x 87 cm) New York, Metropolitan Museum of Art

PLATE 36 EDWARD HICKS *The Peaceable Kingdom*, 1840–45 (44.5 x 60 cm) New York, Brooklyn Museum, Dick S. Ramsay Fund

PLATE 37   Erastus Salisbury Field *Historic Monument of the American Republic* (280 x 400 cm) Springfield, Mass., Museum of Fine Arts (Photo: Sandak, Inc., New York)

PLATE 38   EASTMAN JOHNSON *In the Fields*, 1875 (46 x 70 cm) Detroit, Institute of Arts

Winslow Homer and Thomas Eakins

PLATE 39   WILLIAM MORRIS HUNT *Gloucester Harbor,* 1877 (53.6 x 79.5 cm) Boston, by kind permission of the Museum of Fine
Arts (Gift of the heirs of Mrs. H. N. Slater; Photo: Sandak, Inc., New York)

PLATE 40 THOMAS EAKINS *Max Schmitt in a Single Scull,* 1871 (82 x 116.5 cm) New York, Metropolitan Museum of Art

PLATE 41   THOMAS EAKINS *The Gross Clinic,* 1875 (244 x 198.2 cm) Philadelphia, by kind permission of the Jefferson Medical
College (Photo: A. J. Wyatt)

PLATE 42 WINSLOW HOMER *The Gulf Stream*, 1899 (71.5 x 125 cm) New York, Metropolitan Museum of Art

PLATE 43   WINSLOW HOMER *Breezing Up*, 1876 (61.3 x 96.8 cm) Washington, D.C., National Gallery of Art

61

The Expatriates

PLATE 44   JOHN SINGER SARGENT *El Jaleo*, 1882, Boston, Isabella Stewart Gardner Museum

PLATE 45   JAMES ABBOT MCNEILL WHISTLER *Portrait of Miss Alexander: Harmony in Gray and Green*, 1872–74 (97 x 189 cm) London, Tate Gallery

PLATE 46 JOHN SINGER SARGENT *Madame X,* 1884 (208.6 x 110 cm) New York,
Metropolitan Museum of Art

PLATE 47   MARY CASSATT *Woman and Girl in the Driver's Seat*, 1879 (89.5 x 130.8 cm) Philadelphia, Museum of Art, W. P. Wilstach Collection (Photo: A. J. Wyatt)

PLATE 48   WILLIAM HARNETT *After the Hunt,* 1885 (180.4 x 122 cm) San Francisco, California Palace of the Legion of Honor (Photo: Schopplein)

PLATE 49   JOHN HABERLE *Grandmother's Fireplace*, 1890 (243.9 x 167.6 cm) Detroit, Institute of Arts

The Visionaries

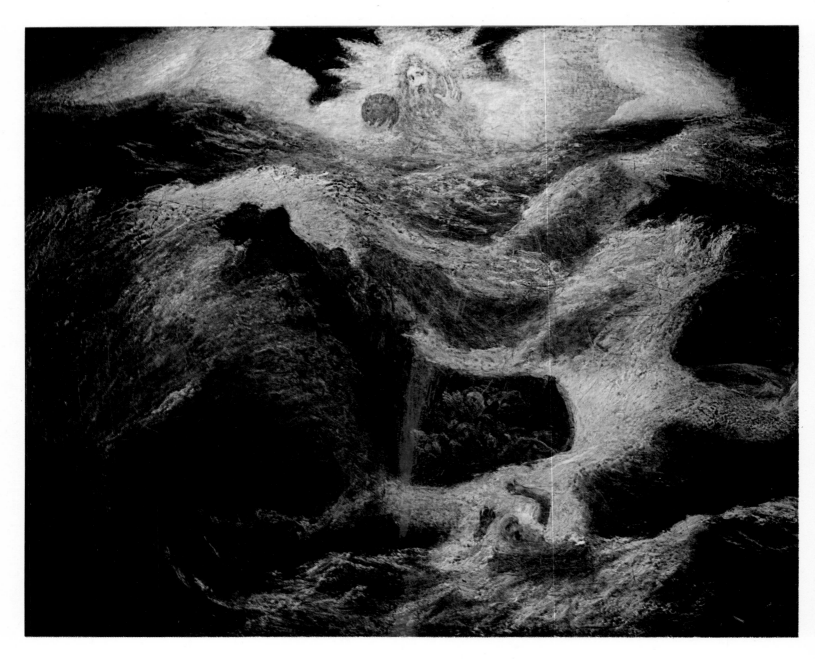

PLATE 50   ALBERT PINKHAM RYDER *Jonah* (67.5 x 85.1 cm) Washington, D.C., National Collection, Smithsonian Institution

PLATE 51   ALBERT PINKHAM RYDER *Toilers of the Sea* (25.4 x 30.5 cm) Andover, Mass., Addison Gallery of American Art, Phillips Academy

PLATE 52   RALPH ALBERT BLAKELOCK *Indian Camp in the Moonlight,* 1889 (67.5 x 85.7 cm) Washington, D. C., National Collection, Smithsonian Institution

70

PLATE 53   JOHN TWACHTMAN *Beneath the Snow,* Chicago, Art Institute of Chicago

PLATE 54   WILLIAM RIMMER *Flight and Pursuit* (45.7 x 66.7 cm) Boston, by kind permission of the Museum of Fine Arts (Gift of Miss Edith Nichols)

72

PLATE 56　WILLIAM MERRITT CHASE *A Friendly Visit*, 1895 (76.8 x 122.5 cm) Washington, D.C., National Gallery of Art (Gift of Chester Dale)

PLATE 57 GEORGE INNESS *The Coming Storm*, 1878 (66 x 99 cm) Buffalo, N. Y., Albright-Knox Art Gallery

75

PLATE 58   CHILDE HASSAM *Rainy Day in Boston*, 1885 (67.3 x 123 cm) Toledo, Ohio, Museum of Art

PLATE 59 WILLIAM PAGE *Portrait of Mrs. Page,* 1860 (153 x 92 cm) Detroit, Institute of Arts

PLATE 60   FRANK DUVENECK *Child's Portrait* (36.8 x 30.5 cm) Detroit, Institute of Arts

THE ARTISTS

WASHINGTON ALLSTON

Born in Georgetown, South Carolina, 1779. Educated in Newport, Rhode Island, and at Harvard University. Took up poetry and painting, in spite of parental objections. Sailed with painter Edward G. Malbone for England in 1801. Pupil of Benjamin West at Royal Academy for several years. Traveled through France, Switzerland, and Italy, with extended stops in Venice, Sienna, Florence. In Rome between 1805 and 1808. Friendships with Washington Irving, Samuel Coleridge, Bertel Thorwaldsen. 1808, returned to Boston, married Ann Channing. Returned to England with wife and pupil Samuel F. B. Morse. In England, 1808-10, where his wife died. In 1818 he returned to Amer-

Allston *Youthful Self-Portrait*, Boston, by kind permission of the Museum of Fine Arts (Gift of Alice Hooper)

ica. Work now lost much of earlier romantic flavor and use of color learned from Venetians. ''Belshazzar's Feast,'' intended as a summary masterpiece, remained uncompleted at death. Settled in Cambridgeport, Massachusetts. Strong influence on younger, romantically inclined artists. Especially helpful to Horatio Greenough and Thomas Crawford. Died in Cambridgeport in 1843.

JOHN JAMES AUDUBON

Born in 1785, the son of a French shipowner and merchant living temporarily in Haiti. As a child taken to Nantes, France, where he began to draw pictures of birds. At seventeen studied briefly in atelier of Jacques Louis David in Paris, his only formal training as an artist. Came to the United States in 1803. At first led life of country gentleman, and was subsequently involved in several unsuccessful business ventures in Kentucky. After 1819 devoted himself entirely to drawing birds.

Wife supported family by working as governess and schoolteacher. In 1820 he conceived the idea of making and publishing drawings of all the birds of America. Went to England in 1826 with over four hundred drawings to be engraved. Sudden popularity and success came when the King purchased a portfolio of plates. Lived for several years in Edinburgh. Returned to the United States in 1831 a famous man. Overseeing the various phases of publishing his *Birds of America* occupied him until the appearance of the final volume in 1839. In 1841 he bought land in New York City on the Hudson River, built a house, and spent remaining years there. In later years wrote and illustrated a book on American quadrupeds with sons John Woodhouse and Victor Gifford. Died in 1851.

ALBERT BIERSTADT

Born at Solingen, near Düsseldorf, Germany, in 1830. Brought as an infant by his family to New Bedford, Massachusetts, where he was brought up and educated. First exhibited painting in 1851 at the New England Art Union in Boston. Exhibited again in Boston in 1853; the same year returned to Düsseldorf to study at Academy under Lessing and Achenbach. Learned to paint in tight, realistic manner. Returned to America in 1857. First trip to western United States in 1858. Paintings exhibited regularly at National Academy. Painted many pictures of the Rocky Mountains in early 1860s. Made a second trip west with his friend Fitz Hugh Ludlow, a journalist and explorer. At peak of his career, received high praise from American and foreign critics. Paintings brought highest prices yet paid an American artist. Traveled with wife to Europe in late 1860s for three years, visited England and much of the Continent. Decorated by several governments. Back in America, painted huge paintings of Yosemite valley. Wife's illness took them to Florida and Nassau, 1877. Next two years in Europe again. House burned down and he began to have financial difficulties. Went to

Audubon *Portrait of His Father*, *J. J. Audubon*, 1841, New York, by kind permission of the American Museum of Natural History

Europe several times between 1883 and 1891. His wife died in Nassau in 1893. He married again in 1894, after which most of his time was spent in New York. Painted until his death in 1902.

GEORGE CALEB BINGHAM

Born in Virginia in 1811. Family moved eight years later to Franklin, Missouri, then in 1823 to Arrow Rock, Saline County. In Boonville, Missouri, 1827-28, apprenticed to a cabinet-maker. Inspired by unknown itinerant portrait painter, Bingham began painting in 1833. By 1836 he was in St. Louis and was married. Went to Philadelphia to study, 1838, then to Baltimore. Sent six paintings to National Academy of Design in 1840. Became involved in presidential campaign of 1840 and from 1841-44 painted portraits in Washington, D. C. Back in St. Louis in 1845, he submitted pictures to American Art Union, New York. Elected to State Legislature in 1846, re-elected 1848. In Columbia, Missouri, and St. Louis during 1850, he was working on series of flatboatmen paintings and began "election series." In 1856 he sailed for Europe, to work in Düsseldorf until 1859. After a brief return trip to Düsseldorf in late 1859, he was between Washington, St. Louis, and Kansas City during 1860. Moved to Jefferson City, 1862, and appointed State Treasurer, a position he held until 1865. Involved in state politics in 1866. Elected school director at Independence, Missouri in 1869. Increasing number of portrait commissions during 1870s. In 1875 he was appointed Adjutant-General of Missouri. Professor of art at University of Missouri, 1877. Remarried after first wife's death. Died in 1879 at Kansas City, Missouri.

WILLIAM MERRITT CHASE

Born in Franklin, Indiana, 1849. As a child made copies after locally printed chromolithographs. Went into Navy briefly; afterward turned to painting. 1867-69, studied under portrait painter Benjamin Hayes in Indianapolis. In 1869 he went to New York to study under L. E. Wilmarth and at the National Academy. Participated in the founding of the Metropolitan Museum of Art, 1870. To St. Louis in 1871, where local citizens gathered funds to send him abroad. Entered the Academy in Munich, 1872. Worked under Alexander Wagner and Karl von Piloti. Came under influence of Wilhelm Leibl. Shared studio with Frank Duveneck, 1875; John Twachtman was also a student there. Painting mostly indoors, portrait commissions. 1877, to Venice for nine months with Duveneck and Twachtman. Began to paint more out of doors. In 1878 he returned to New York, took up teaching position at Art Students League. Enjoyed informal intimacy of artist life with others working at Tenth Street Studio. 1881, revisited Europe and traveled to Spain, Belgium, France, Holland. In 1885 he met Whistler in London. They agreed to paint each other's portrait. Became president of the Society of American Artists. Taught at Brooklyn Art School, 1890, then at Shinnecock, Long Island. Opened the Chase School in New York, 1896, but forced to close studio in 1897 due to

BINGHAM *Self-Portrait*, 1877, Kansas City, William Rockhill Nelson Gallery of Art

financial crisis. Became head of schools at Pennsylvania Academy in Philadelphia in 1897. Back and forth to Europe in 1890s. Joined group of the "Ten" in 1902. Died in New York, 1916.

FREDERICK EDWIN CHURCH

Born in Hartford, Connecticut, in 1826. Studied briefly with painters Alexander Hamilton Emmons and Benjamin Hutchins Coe, 1842–43. Was taken on as Thomas Cole's only pupil from 1844 to 1846. He exhibited paintings for the first time at National Academy of Design. Around 1847 or 1848 moved to New York City. He exhibited regularly at National Academy and American Art Union. Accepted William James Stillman as pupil. In 1849 he was elected to full membership in National Academy. Trip through Vermont and New Hampshire, 1850, and first visit to Maine coast. Took on second pupil, Jervis McEntee. 1851, trip through Virginia, North Carolina, Kentucky, and upper Mississippi River valley; later to the Catskills and the Maine coast. In 1852 elected an officer of National Academy. 1853, first trip to South America. 1854, Nova Scotia and Maine. Continued to exhibit at National Academy. Second trip to South America in 1857. To Newfoundland and Labrador during summer of 1859. Married Isabel Carnes in 1860; sketched in Catskills, Mount Desert Island, Maine. Moved to property acquired in Hudson, New York. In the Catskills, 1862 and 1863. 1866-67, had major paintings on tour and an exhibition abroad. Left for France late 1867. In London, then on extensive trip through Near East during 1868. Collaboration on painting in Rome with Jervis McEntee and George Healy. Returned to New York, 1869, sketching in Catskills. 1870, began construction of Moorish villa "Olana" at Hudson. Painted at Hudson and in Maine during the seventies. Little artistic activity after 1880. In Mexico, 1883–85, again in '89, '90, '93, and '99. 1900, returned to New York in poor health. Died at home of friend and patron William H. Osborn.

THOMAS COLE

Born at Bolton-le-Moor, Lancashire, England, in 1801. Early years of schooling in Chester, England. Apprenticed to a calico designer and an engraver. 1819, came with family to America, settled in Philadelphia. Further experience in wood engraving. Brief visit to West Indies. Returned to Philadelphia, took walking trip to Steubenville, Ohio, where family had moved. Decided to become a painter around 1820. Next few years was itinerant portrait painter in Ohio. Disappointments led him to return to Philadelphia in 1823. Spent some time at Pennsylvania Academy of Fine Arts, impressed with landscapes by Thomas Birch and Thomas Doughty. Along with Doughty one of the founders of the Hudson River School. By 1825, in New York, sold landscapes readily. Reputation quickly established. In 1826, one of founding members of the National Academy of Design. Increasingly withdrew from city life to work in the Catskills. Paintings bought by prominent collectors Daniel Wadsworth and Robert Gilmor. Gilmor provided funds for long-delayed trip to Europe. Quick trip to Niagara Falls before leaving for England in 1829. Visited Royal Academy, where he was impressed with landscapes by Claude, Gaspard, Poussin, and Turner. Went to Louvre in Paris, traveled through Rhone valley. By 1831 in Florence, then on to Rome, occupying a studio once used by Claude Lorrain. Visited and sketched at Naples and Paestum. 1832, returned to New York. Patronized by Lumen Reed, who commissioned famous *Course of Empire* series. Second trip to Europe in 1841-42, traveling from England to Sicily, sketching and studying old masters. New popularity in United States from circulation of engravings after his works. Took on his only pupil, Frederick E. Church, in 1844. Died in New York, 1848.

COLE *Self-Portrait*, New York, by kind permission of the New-York Historical Society

THOMAS DOUGHTY

Born in Philadelphia in 1793. One of the first American painters to devote himself to landscape. As a youth apprenticed to a leather currier. Turned about 1820 to career as an artist. Rapid success followed. Elected member of Pennsylvania Academy of Fine Arts in 1824. Exhibited at National Academy of Design, New York, 1826. Was painting in Pennsylvania, Maryland, New York, and New England. Between 1826 and 1830 in Boston. 1830, began publication in Philadelphia of a magazine illustrated with lithographs after his works. Between 1832 and 1837 back in Boston, teaching painting and drawing. 1837, to England for two years. After his return, worked in Newburgh, New York. After 1840 moved to New York City. Second painting trip to England, Ireland, and France in 1845-46. Works became widely popular, exhibited often in the United States and abroad. Many paintings exhibited across the country through the American Art-Union. Later work tended to repeat stock formulas. Died in 1856.

ASHER BROWN DURAND

Born in 1796 at Jefferson Village (now Maplewood), New Jersey. His father, a watchmaker and silversmith, taught him engraving. From 1812 to 1817 he was apprenticed to engraver Peter Maverick of Newark. Became partner in firm for three years. Did engravings for gift book annuals, bank notes, and other commercial documents. The art patron Luman Reed encouraged him to turn to painting. Took up landscape painting in 1830s. Sketched woods near Hoboken, New Jersey. Under Thomas Cole's influence soon traveled up the Hudson valley and to the White Mountains, Catskills, Adirondacks, and Berkshires. 1840, through financial assistance of Jonathan Sturges, went abroad with painters Thomas Rossiter, John Casilear, and John F. Kensett. Toured galleries in London, Paris, Rome, and Florence. His work became popular with New York collectors; paintings had special precision and clarity due to early training as an engraver. Published in *The Crayon*, 1855, his "Letters on Landscape Painting," outlining his approach to art. A founding member of the National Academy of Design, active in New York art circles. Exhibited regularly at Academy between 1826 and early 1870s. Second president, after resignation of Samuel F. B. Morse, from 1845-61. 1869, retired in New Jersey, where he died in 1886.

THOMAS EAKINS

Born in Philadelphia, 1844. Studied drawing at the Pennsylvania Academy of Fine Arts and anatomy at Jefferson Medical College during the early 1860s. Developed lifelong interest in science and mathematics. Sailed for France in 1866, entered Gerome's class at the Ecole des Beaux Arts. In 1869 went to Spain, where he admired seventeenth-century Spanish painting, notably that of Velázquez. Returned to Philadelphia, 1872; remained until 1888. Painted home scenes, members of his family at work and play, series of boating pictures on Skuylkill River. Became engaged to Katherine Crowell in 1872. Painted *The Gross Clinic*, 1875. Began teaching at the Pennsylvania Academy without pay. 1879, made professor of anatomy at the Academy. In the same year his wife died. The following year joined the Society of American Artists. 1884, married his pupil, Susan Hannah MacDowell. Did photographic experiments on movements of men and animals. Forced to resign from Pennsylvania Academy for allowing a male model to pose in the nude. Loyal pupils organized the Philadelphia Art Students League to continue studying under Eakins. Went to New Jersey, to meet Walt Whitman and paint his portrait. Taught at National Academy of Design in New York, 1888-94. 1902, unanimously elected to the National Academy, made an Academician two months later. Died in Philadelphia, 1916.

ERASTUS SALISBURY FIELD

Born at Leverett, Massachusetts, in 1805. Largely self-taught as an artist, although briefly a pupil of Samuel F. B. Morse in 1824. Most of career an itinerant painter in western Massachusetts. Early portraits display careful handling of paint, rich sense of color, and stiff mannerisms in portraits. Developed shorthand technique that permitted him to finish a full-size portrait in one day. In 1841 Field went to New York. Listed during next several years as painter, portraitist, and artist at various locations in New York. Made a return trip to Massachusetts in 1845. Probably spent part of his time in New York learning about photography. After return to Massachusetts in 1849 a number of portraits were based on photographs. 1854, opened a studio in Palmer, posing his sitters before a camera, but ensuing paintings lost some of earlier vitality and brightness. After death of wife in 1959, painted increasingly fewer portraits, turning more to biblical and historical scenes, many based on engravings. For many years his early work went unattributed, but since 1942

nearly 300 works have been identified as his. Died at Plumtrees, Massachusetts, in 1900.

MARTIN JOHNSON HEADE

Born 1819 in Buck's County, Pennsylvania. Some early instruction in painting from portraitist Thomas Hicks. Lifetime of travel began before he was twenty, with a trip to Italy, France, and England. In 1843 he set up a studio in New York. Early work included some portraits, also landscapes in the Hudson River School manner. Traveled to St. Louis and Chicago during the 1850s, and in years following painted in Philadelphia, Providence, Newburyport and Boston, Massachusetts, and along the Maine coast. Met Rev. J. C. Fletcher, who was interested in natural history; took trip with Fletcher to South America in 1863. Hoped to publish a book on hummingbirds with chromolithographed illustrations, which project he dedicated in 1865 to Emperor Don Pedro II of Brazil. He was never able to find a publisher, although he tried in both England and the United States. In later years traveled again to South America, and also to the California coast. Friendship during seventies and eighties with Frederick E. Church, whose studio he regularly used in New York. Continued travel to various parts of America. In his sixties he married and settled in Florida, where he died in 1904.

EDWARD HICKS

Born 1780 at Newtown, Pennsylvania. One of best-known painters of the nineteenth century. Son of an Episcopalian mother who died while he was a child and a Quaker father too impoverished to raise him. Brought up by the Twining family. Showed little inclination for higher education. At thirteen was apprenticed to a coachmaker. By 1801, in Milford, Pennsylvania, a partner in a coachmaking and painting business. Began to paint street, shop, and tavern signs. In 1811 he

HEADE *Twilight on the Salt Marshes*, Boston, by kind permission of the Museum of Fine Arts, Maxim Karolik Fund

settled in Newtown, where he expanded the painting branch of his business. Output became so popular that he took on a number of assistants. Active throughout his career as a Quaker preacher. Became interested in theme of The Peaceable Kingdom because of bitter schism among the Quakers. Painted nearly fifty versions of the subject, often including scripture painted around the edges. Most of paintings were based on prints, but possessed their own originality. Although a successful artist, he continued painting signs. Died in Pennsylvania in 1849.

WINSLOW HOMER

Born in Boston, 1836. Family moved to Cambridge, Massachusetts, around 1842. Was apprenticed at an early age to J. H. Bufford, Boston lithographer. Left Bufford in 1857 to begin free-lance illustration; his work first appeared in *Harper's Weekly*, to which he contributed regularly until 1875. Moved in 1859 to New York, which remained his winter home until the 1880s. Attended drawing school in Brooklyn around 1860; the next year studied in night school, National Academy of Design. Covered Lincoln's inauguration in 1861; later that year covered the Army of the Potomac outside Washington. Studied painting briefly with Frederic Rondel. 1862, on the Peninsular Campaign in Virginia at beginning of Civil War. Between 1863 and 1865 made occasional trips to the Front, produced series of war paintings and illustrations for publication in *Harper's*. Elected Associate of National Academy, the next year Academician. Sailed for France in 1866, stayed for a year; remained active as book and magazine illustrator. Summer of 1873 in Gloucester, Massachusetts, where he made first watercolor series. In 1875 he was in Virginia, painting oils of Negro subjects. Upstate New York, 1878. Returned to Gloucester for summer of 1880, when he returned to watercolors. In England, 1881, where he settled at Tynemouth on North Sea coast. Returned to America in 1882; the next year did series of large watercolors based on English sketches. 1883, he settled at Prout's Neck, Maine. Series of watercolors at Prout's Neck, 1887-89; several etchings during same period. There are no oils dated from these years. During the period 1889-1903 he traveled to the Adirondacks, Florida, Quebec, Nassau, and Bermuda. Long illness during summer of 1906; no works dated between late 1905 and late 1908. He suffered a paralytic stroke in 1908, although he was still able to paint. Died in 1910 at Prout's Neck.

WILLIAM MORRIS HUNT

Born in 1824. Attended Harvard University, but did not receive a degree. Family sent him to Paris in the 1840s. Entered Couture's studio, became interested in Millet, near whom he lived and worked for two years. Also studied in Rome and at The Academy in Düsseldorf. Returned to America in 1855. First lived in Boston, then at Newport, Rhode Island. Joined by his most important pupil, John LaFarge. Civil War forced him to move back to Boston, where he settled about 1862. Turned increasingly to portraiture, with which he was successful. Persuaded wealthy friends to buy paintings by the Barbizon painters. Second visit to Europe in 1866. His studio in Boston burned in 1872, destroying most of his work, including a commissioned portrait of President Lincoln. Began teaching class in new Boston studio, which turned out to be a success. Taught primarily in charcoal, used for most of his own sketches. In 1877 he spent the summer on Cape Ann, producing misty, impressionistic landscapes. The next year received commission to decorate state capitol building at Albany, New York. Poor construction and finishing of the dome caused murals to be destroyed not long after completion. Died 1879.

GEORGE INNESS

Born 1825 near Newburgh, New York. Family moved within a year to New York City, and in 1829 to Newark, New Jersey, where he was educated and brought up. Took painting and drawing lessons from an art teacher named Barker. In 1841 he worked as a map engraver with a New York

firm. Soon gave up engraving for sketching directly from nature. Married about age eighteen to Delia Miller, who died a few months later. Brief study with Regis Gignoux, 1845; exhibited at National Academy of Design and American Art Union. Opened his own studio in New York. 1847, sailed to Europe, spent a brief time in England and Italy. In 1850 he married Elizabeth Hart, and they went abroad. Studied and painted in Florence for two years. 1853, elected Associate Member of National Academy of Design. Went to Europe again, where he was influenced by Corot and Fontainbleau school. Returned home in 1855. Settled in Medfield, Massachusetts. During early sixties was painting in the Adirondacks, Catskills, Berkshires, and North Conway, New Hampshire. In 1864 moved to Eagleswood, New Jersey, then in 1867 to Brooklyn. 1870, sailed to Europe; in Rome for two years. Returned to Boston because of fire at his Boston dealers. Back in Normandy, France, during 1873-74; returned to New York in

HOMER *Puff of Wind at Long Branch During the Swimming Hour,* New York, New York Public Library

1875. Moved to Montclair, New Jersey, in 1878. Summers in the 1880s were spent in Connecticut, Nantucket, Niagara Falls, and upstate New York. Early 1890s, trips to Florida, California, and Canada. 1894, to Europe; visited Scotland, where he died suddenly at the little town of Bridge-of-Allan.

EASTMAN JOHNSON

Born in Augusta, Maine, 1824, where he spent his youth. 1840, went to Boston for lithographic training, probably at Bufford's (publisher of Fitz Hugh Lane and later teacher of Winslow Homer). Returned home and began artistic career as a portraitist. 1845-46, in Washington, D. C., where he established his reputation. Invited to Boston by the poet H. W. Longfellow to do his family's portraits. Left for Europe in 1849 to study at Düsseldorf. Struck up close friendship with influential teacher there, Emmanuel Leutze. Stayed three years, making careful studies after old masters. Dutch influence important to his style at this time. After some traveling, returned to America in 1855 because of mother's death. Traveled through the northeast and midwestern United States. Followed Union Army during Civil War. First mature genre paintings during the 1860s. Style combined tight handling of Düsseldorf manner with looser freedom of Dutch painting. Increasing consciousness of light in paintings of the seventies. Scenes of cranberry pickers on Nantucket Island done in mid-seventies. During 1880s returned to doing more remunerative portraits, not equal to genre pictures. Painted series of United States Presidents, which brought a number of commissions. Career ended about 1887 with last major genre pieces. Spent last period of his life painting portraits. Died in 1906.

FITZ HUGH LANE

Born in Gloucester, Massachusetts, in 1804. At age of two, paralyzed in legs, probably from polio. As a result was forced to use crutches for rest of his life. Educated in local schools, spent some time drawing along nearby coast. Work came to attention of William Pendleton, best-known lithographer in Boston at the time. Was apprenticed to Pendleton in 1832, spent most of next decade in Boston. Saw and was influenced by Robert Salmon's paintings. Joined a fellow artist, John W. A. Scott, in forming their own lithographic firm in 1845. Was painting both in Boston and Gloucester at this time. Beginning in 1848 and continuing regularly into the early 1860s Lane made cruises with his friends to the Maine coast. There was a change in his style from dark, somber colors and heavy application of paint, usually for stormy scenes, to pale, cool colors and thin glazing of paint. Subjects now more quiet, detached, poetic. His work in Maine concentrated primarily in area of Penobscot Bay and Mount Desert Island. Late paintings and lithographs have increasing openness, economy, and serenity. Never married. Died in Gloucester, 1865.

WILLIAM SIDNEY MOUNT

Born at Setauket, New York, in 1807, where he spent most of his life. Brought up in nearby Stony Brook. 1824, went to New York, apprenticed to his brother Henry, a sign painter. Became a pupil in 1826 at school of the National Academy. 1832, elected an Academician. Stayed in New York until 1837, when he returned to Stony Brook. A lover of the out-of-doors, also a musician. Bored with portraiture, he delighted in recording the activities of his friends and neighbors and made paintings of rural scenes and everyday life in the area around his home town. These anecdotal farm scenes were not well received by critics, who expected more genteel subjects. Encouraged by collectors Luman Reed and Robert Gilmor. He painted carefully and slowly, using pencil and oil sketches before turning to canvas. Production slowed markedly in later years. Highly religious, he said he had spiritual communications with Rembrandt and other old masters in the last years of his life. Died at the house of his brother in Setauket in 1868.

WILLIAM PAGE

Born 1811 in Albany, New York. At age of nine moved to New York City with his family. 1822, talent for drawing won him a prize at the American Academy. 1825, worked briefly in New York law firm. Soon after entered studio of James Herring. Also studied with Samuel F. B. Morse. Joined drawing class at National Academy of Design in 1826. The next year awarded a prize for excellence in life drawing and exhibited his first painting. During next few years was active painting portraits and historical subjects in New York and Massachusetts. 1833, married and opened a studio in New York City. Elected a director of the Ameri-

PEALE *The Artist in His Gallery*, Philadelphia, by kind permission of the Pennsylvania Academy of Fine Arts

can Academy in 1835; two years later became an Academician. Moved to Boston in 1843, but lack of commissions forced his return to New York in 1847. Left for Europe in 1850; made copies after Titian. Returned to New York and took quarters in Tenth Street Studio building in 1867. Taught at National Academy. Elected president of Academy in 1871. In later years painted a few portraits, many based on photographs. Died at his home in Tottenville, Staten Island, New York, in 1885.

CHARLES WILLSON PEALE

Born in Maryland, 1741. An inventor, painter, saddler, scientist, museum proprietor, soldier, writer, and naturalist. Rudimentary education in local schools. Youthful apprenticeship to a saddler. Early crude attempts at portraiture, landscape, and sign painting. 1750s to Philadelphia, where he visited studios of local artists, received some instruction from portrait painter John Hesselius. Increasing range of talents: upholstery, silversmithing, harnessmaking, watch repairing. 1765, sailed to Boston, visited John Smibert's studio. Went on to Newburyport, Massachusetts. Back in Boston, saw John Singleton Copley and his works, began painting portraits in Copley's manner. Left to study in London, 1767. Received some instruction from Benjamin West. During two years in London elected to Society of Artists. Returned to Annapolis, Maryland, in 1769. Annual visits to Philadelphia until 1775 for portrait commissions. 1776, settled in Philadelphia. Increasing attention to projects other than painting in latter part of career, especially creation of a museum. 1792, museum moved to American Philosophical Society, and in 1802 to the Pennsylvania State House. In later years he turned to inventing. 1805, one of founders of Pennsylvania Academy of Fine Arts. Wrote several books between 1797 and 1812. Married three times, had many children. Died in Philadelphia in 1827.

RAPHAEL PEALE

Born in 1774 in Annapolis, Maryland, the son of the versatile painter Charles Willson Peale. Received most of instruction in painting from his father. Helped establish museum of natural history in Philadelphia. Went to Baltimore in late 1790s; with brother Rembrandt attempted to start a portrait gallery of distinguished persons. Like his father, experimented in science and patented several inventions. 1795, drew Washington from life; was also painting still lifes and *trompe l'oeil* paintings. Around 1800, returned to Philadelphia, where he advertised himself as a portrait painter. 1803, in Norfolk, Virginia, seeking commissions; 1804, went south on a painting trip with Rembrandt. Around 1815 devoted himself increasingly to still-life painting. Never went abroad, though work shows an apparent awareness of seventeenth-century Dutch painting. Died in 1825.

JOHN QUIDOR

Born in Tappan, New York, in 1801. About 1811 family moved to New York City, where Quidor

QUIDOR *Youthful Self-Portrait*, 1828, Newark, N. J., Newark Museum

RYDER *Self-Portrait*, c. 1883, New York, by kind permission of the Kennedy Galleries

spent most of his life. Brief apprenticeship sometime between 1814 and 1822 under the portraitist John Wesley Jarvis. A fellow pupil was painter Henry Inman, although neither teacher nor colleague appears to have influenced Quidor. Earliest picture is dated 1823. First paintings exhibited in 1828 at National Academy. Received mixed reception. About 1830 Charles Loring Elliott, a portraitist, and his friend Thomas Bangs Thorpe became his pupils. 1833, exhibited in American Academy of Arts and at the Boston Athenaeum. Address listed as New York until 1836. Movements for next few years unclear. Painted several large biblical scenes, abandoning literary subjects from Irving and Cooper of preceding years. Exhibited in National Academy in 1847. Returned to painting in 1855 after lapse of sixteen years without dated works. Stylistic changes from early period include greater use of thin glazes, pervading amber tones, and in last works nervous calligraphy. In 1856 did second versions of earlier paintings, which were not as successful. Last pictures in 1867-68. Moved about 1868 to home of his daughter in Jersey City Heights, New Jersey, where he died in 1881.

ALBERT PINKHAM RYDER

Born in New Bedford, Massachusetts, in 1847. Began painting landscapes without any formal training. Moved to New York around 1870, where he stayed most of his life. Studied briefly at the National Academy of Design, and under engraver and portraitist William E. Marshall. Exhibited at National Academy in 1873. In 1877 was one of founders of Society of American Artists, where he exhibited between 1878 and 1887. Made four brief trips abroad in 1873, 1882, 1887, and 1896. After 1880 became increasingly imaginative, took up literary and biblical themes. Worked on many of these paintings for years. Painted instinctively, without much technical knowledge. Many of his works have since discolored or cracked as a result. Seldom visited museums or dealers' galleries, although he did admit an admiration for Corot. Work began to meet with some favor in the 1880s, although he was generally unappreciated and misunderstood. Worked on series of moonlight marines called *Toilers of the Sea*. A falling off in creativity about 1900, when he was in his early fifties. Seldom exhibited after 1887, and there are few pictures dated after this period. Strong measure of recognition by younger artists, who included several of his works in the Armory Show of 1913. After serious illness, died on Long Island in 1917.

ROBERT SALMON

Born in Whitehaven, Cumberland, England, in 1775. Early training unknown. Was exhibiting at Royal Academy, London, in 1802. Arrived in Liverpool in 1806, painted views of city and shipping on Mersey River for four years. Left for Greenock, Scotland, in 1811. Joined Society for the Promotion of Arts and Sciences in Greenock and exhibited ten paintings. Helped found a similar institution in Glasgow in 1821. Returned to Liverpool in 1822. Completed nearly eighty paintings in the next three years. Exhibited six paintings in the Academy of the Liverpool Royal Institution. Returned to Greenock (1825) for another two years. From 1826 to 1828 in London, Southampton, North Shields. Exhibited two paintings at the British Institute, London in 1827. Sailed in 1828 from Liverpool to New York, and immediately went on to Boston. Painted several large theater backdrops. Soon gained patronage of city's most prominent merchants and citizens. Occupied a studio overlooking Boston Harbor. Painted Boston harbor, coastline and outer islands. Recorded thousandth painting in 1839. In 1842 he returned to England, where he died in 1844.

JOHN SINGER SARGENT

Born in Florence, 1856. Decided to become an artist at age of thirteen. In 1874 he entered the studio of Carolus Duran, who was influenced by Velázquez. Developed a technique of spontaneity and immense facility. 1876, came to America for first time for Centennial celebration in Philadelphia. First major paintings of Spanish subjects were the result of a trip to Spain in 1880. Later, in Venice, studied Tiepolo and Tintoretto. His painting of Madame X created an immediate storm in Paris Salon of 1884. Friendship with Henry James, Edwin Austin Abbey, Robert Louis Stevenson. 1887, came to United States with several portrait commissions. In 1889 he returned to England. Experimented with Impressionism. Received a commission to decorate Boston Public Library, a welcome change from portraiture, although there were a large number of portraits in late nineties. Traveled frequently throughout Europe to sketch. Late in life he gave up portraiture for the most part to do watercolors and charcoal-pencil sketches. Completed decorations of Boston Museum of Fine Arts, and, just after the war, murals for Widener Library at Harvard University. A conscientious teacher in academy schools. A fresh brightness appears in his late watercolors. His last ten years spent almost equally between Boston and London. Died in 1925.

GILBERT STUART

Born near Newport, Rhode Island, 1755, and spent early years there. About 1769 became pupil of Cosmo Alexander, a visiting portraitist from Scotland. In 1772 accompanied Alexander to Edinburgh, but forced to return home shortly after. With approach of American Revolution, left for London in 1775. Went to live and work with Benjamin West from 1777 to 1782. Then opened his own studio, received many commissions, and achieved success in face of competition from notable painters like Gainsborough, Reynolds, and Romney. Based technique on their style and compositions. Inept at business matters, harassed by debts. Went to Dublin, for several years, then returned to New York. Constantly employed as portraitist in New York, Philadelphia, and Boston, where he settled in 1805. Wide recognition for his famous portraits of Washington. Gradually abandoned rich and florid English style; portraits accordingly lost some of earlier power and liveliness. Later years beset by financial difficulties and poor health. Died in 1828.

JOHN VANDERLYN

Born in Kingston, New York, in 1775, the grandson of the primitive limner and house painter Pieter Vanderlyn. Employed as a youth by a New York printseller. Took drawing lessons from Archibald Robertson. About 1794 copied portraits by Gilbert Stuart, gained attention from Aaron Burr, who paid for his further instruction from Stuart and for a trip to Europe. 1796, left for Paris; returned to New York in 1801. Painted portraits and first landscapes, one of the first of which was a view of Niagara Falls. 1803, second trip to Europe, most of time in Paris, briefly in Rome. Awarded a Gold Medal in 1808 by Napoleon. Returned to America in 1815. Unable to compete with new artistic ideas and younger emerging artists, his popularity began to wane. Friends provided money to build a large rotunda for exhibition of his Versailles panorama. He was plagued by debts, bad luck, mismanagement, and the longstanding frustration of trying to obtain a commission from the U. S. Government to decorate the Capitol rotunda. It was finally granted in 1837, when he was sixty-two. Now worn out and embittered, he fled to Paris, taking eight years to finish the work. When installed at last, the painting met with devastating criticism. In last years reduced to begging. Died alone and penniless in a rented tavern room in native town of Kingston.

JAMES ABBOTT McNEILL WHISTLER

Born 1834 in Lowell, Massachusetts. Taken at an early age to St. Petersburg, Russia, where his father had a job as an engineer. Childhood spent in Europe. At age of fifteen, returned to America, spent a few years at West Point, although he did not graduate. Worked for a few months with the U.S. Coast and Geodetic Survey, where he learned techniques of drawing and etching. 1855, in Paris, became pupil of Charles Gleyre, a follower of Ingres. Soon met artistic revolutionaries Courbet, Monet, Manet, and Degas. Also attracted to early Barbizon work. Slowly began to move away from orthodox realism in 1860s, when he began to enjoy his first success. Friendship with the Pre-Raphaelites, especially Rossetti, around mid-sixties. Began his *Nocturne* series in Valparaiso,

CHASE *Whistler's Portrait*, 1885, New York, Metropolitan Museum of Art (Gift of William H. Walker)

VANDERLYN *Self-Portrait*, New York, Metropolitan Museum of Art (Gift of Ann S. Stephens in the name of her mother)

South America, in 1866, under influence of Japanese prints. In London during Franco-Prussian War, 1870-71, with many French artists, including Monet. New attention to portraiture; period of great productivity. After several exhibitions his reputation slowly advanced. In 1877 Ruskin made his famous attack accusing Whistler of "flinging a pot of paint in the public's face." A libel suit and trial followed. It was a victory for Whistler, establishing the idea of "art for art's sake," but he was bankrupt from having to pay for trial. Escaped to Venice, 1879-80, when there was a major turning point in his work. This was a productive period of pastels and etchings in impressionistic manner, and he conducted a personal publicity campaign to restore his reputation. Enjoyed a new prominence after return to London. Began writing ideas on art, given as "The Ten O'Clock Lectures," in 1885. Friendship with William Merritt Chase. Large Paris retrospective exhibition in 1892. New series of etchings in Paris. Further ideas on art published in *The Gentle Art of Making Enemies*. After his wife's death in 1896, he traveled extensively. Died in 1903.

List of Illustrations

Printed in Italy by A. Mondadori - Verona